Boners in the News

by

JULIET LOWELL

ILLUSTRATIONS BY
RICHARD BENNETT

pb
SPECIAL

NEW YORK / 1966

Foreword

The newspapers exude such a picture of gloom that I think we should be grateful for any fun we can find in the press. That's why, while traveling around the country for two and a half years on my lecture tour, I took my scissors, read the papers, and clipped the Boners from the News, so that you too could share the FUN.

News Flashes

* * *

Lady's leather handbag left in my car while parked on State St. yesterday. Owner can have same by calling at my office, proving the property and paying for this ad. If she will square me with my wife for its being there, I will pay for the ad.

Weather Forecast: Thunder showers Friday probably followed by Saturday.

JOHNSTOWN DEMOCRAT

Our paper carried the notice last week that Mr. Hamilton Ferris is a defective in the police force. This was a typographical error. Mr. Ferris is a detective in the police farce.

KANSAS BULLETIN

The shortest marriage in the history of Sacramento County was revealed today with the filing of an annulment action by Gust Skarles against Mary Ellen Skarles.

The couple married on June 22nd. Six hours after the ceremony they were separated. Skarles asks for the annulment on the ground his wife refused to live with him.

The Skarles have four children.

SACRAMENTO BEE

THE STANVILLE COURIER

Mrs. Tamley, 5 Main Street, takes pleasure in announcing that her parking space, temporarily under repair, is now ready for constant use. Open all night. Everybody welcome.

There are pants which open and close at such definite hours of the day that it is possible to tell fairly accurate time by them.

SIOUX CITY TRIBUNE

The prices of our coats and vests are being reduced this week and our pants will come down tomorrow.

A jolly bunch of our young people went on a kodaking expedition Sunday that resulted in many exposures and a very enjoyable time.

FOUR GIRLS ACCUSE HIM AS FATHER OF THEIR BABIES.

Walter Anuzie, 26 years old, 2011 Cullerton Street, was arraigned in the Court of Domestic Relations yesterday on the complaints of four young women, each of whom alleged that he was the father of her child. Anuzie is an employee of a baby carriage factory.

CHICAGO TRIBUNE

The Rev. C. Rankin Barnes, executive secretary of the National Department of Christian Social Service, declared here this afternoon in an address at the conference of the Provincial Commission on Christian Social Service that instruction in marriage should begin in childhood and not be confined to the period immediately prior to the time when the organ begins to play.

THE NEW YORK TIMES

The Post Office Department is never questioned. Every person who presents a letter for mailing is fully confident that it will be safely carried to its destruction.

THE OBSERVER, MICHIGAN LAKE

John C. Myers, city clerk, yesterday issued a marriage license to Miss Lela M. Smith and Kenneth L. Johnson. They plan to be married within a few days. The bride is the daughter of Mrs. Estalla LaBeef and a native of Phoenix. Mr. Johnson is the son of Mr. and Mrs. Frank Johnson and a chauffeur.

SYRACUSE HERALD

PAUL DONNELYS IMPROVE

Condition of Husband and Bride Termed Satisfactory

The condition of Paul Donnely and his bride, the former Virginia George, actress, continued satisfactory today at St. Luke's Hospital.

Mr. Donnely suffered a nervous breakdown and was advised to enter the hospital on his return from his honeymoon in Florida a few weeks ago. His bride is also convalescing from nervous exhaustion and fatigue. Neither is in a dangerous condition.

KANSAS CITY
STAR

The slowest time ever made by a railroad train was on the passenger train Tuesday from Fremont to West Point. A couple took the train at Fremont, telegraphed to a minister to meet them at Pebble Creek where they were married aboard the cars. Before the train reached West Point the couple had a son born that weighed 12 pounds. The whole distance traveled was 32 miles.

OMAHA
WORLD-HERALD

Married women compromise forty percent of the school teacher personnel in Honolulu, T.H. the total out of 2,646 employed.

PORTLAND
PRESS HERALD

SYRACUSE
JOURNAL

Lord Northesk will be Peggy's fifth husband. In her matrimonial ventures she has been a countess but she has never been a lady.

THE LONDON
DAILY TIMES

His face was a striking one, and even without his clothes, people would have turned to look at him.

Mrs. Natalie Vankyser wants a divorce from her husband. Thirty years ago he left home to buy a loaf of bread and hasn't returned. Mrs. Vankyser is pretty sure he has deserted her.

There has been an increase of maternity work, doubtless due to unemployment. There isn't much to do on the island in winter outside of fishing, anyway, and when that fails the natives find it kind of tiresome just sitting around and waiting for the mail boat to get in.

NANTUCKET PRESS ANNUAL TOWN REPORT

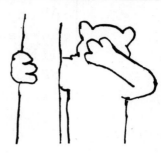

Bear drives camper out of tent in his pajama top. He climbs tree with bear behind.

Montague Love, the leading man, threw out his chest three inches and followed it across the stage!

Albany, June 1 (AP)— An extensive campaign to rid New York State of ten caterpillars took shape today under direction of Agriculture Commissioner Eyck.

The fire was put out before any damage was done by the local fire department.

Mr. Ogden lectured today on "Insect Pests"; a large number were present.

HARRISBURG CHRONICLE

A large night-blooming Cereus Plant, owned by Mrs. Thomson, put forth two large buds which bloomed last Saturday evening. Mrs. Thomson will be glad to show her night bloomers to anyone who cares to see them.

NEW YORK HERALD TRIBUNE

Miss Fanny Fish, our popular soprano, will sing, and the Reverend Thomas's Sermon will be, "Is this Hell?"

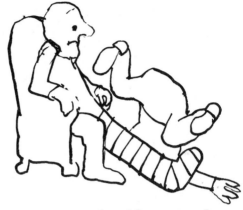

Accidents and
Medical Reports

*   *   *

The city ambulance department had 16 calls from the French Village and the encampment at the Exhibition Grounds of the Canadian Corps Reunion men Saturday and Sunday. Most of the ambulances carried away men who had collapses from over-erection or other causes.

TORONTO
MAIL AND EMPIRE

Dr. Newgass' speech on "How to Keep Fit" will be cancelled tonight, due to his being sick in bed.

Hobart Jones has been in Hutchinson since last Tuesday where he went to have a tooth extracted. They found the tooth so imbedded in the bum that it was necessary to take him to the hospital.

Miss Wilma Enid Martin of Miamitown, Ohio, who underwent an appendicitis operation for removal of her tonsils was dismissed today.

IRON NEWS

Mr. C. M. Hooch was taken ill on Tuesday evening and has been confined to his bed under the care of his doctor. It makes it bad to think that he and his wife are both in bed at the same time.

DOVER
STATE SENTINEL

Sherman was shot, stabbed, kicked and beaten into insensibility in the furious melee, but was not seriously hurt, according to physicians at Polyclinic Hospital.

NEW YORK
WORLD

On finding a man uncon-
scious always smell the
breath — sometimes you
will be agreeably sur-
prised.

As to the heart condition,
a result of the accident,
Dr. Stahl stated that while
she will probably always
have this ailment, it will
not, in his opinion, al-
ways be permanent.

Sam Hoskins accidentally shot himself while hunting. One of the wounds is fatal, but his friends are glad to hear that the other one is not serious.

Under general anesthesia, I did a Caldwell LUC and this cured him of his nose bleeding and so improved his general condition that he got rid of his nervousness and also his wife.

Fifty-two others were reported as injured by ambulance surgeons at the scene of the accident.

~~~~~~~~~~~~

AMERICAN
MEDICAL JOURNAL

Disturbed sleep in infants may be due to lack of vitamin B_1, D, G, and P. P.

BLOOMINGTON
PANTAGRAPH

Joseph Ott, farmer of near Fairbury, was in St. Joseph's hospital Saturday night with a fractured Saturday night with a fractured Saturday afternoon at his farm.

AMERICAN
HEART JOURNAL

October, 1931—Prognosis of Angina Pectoris, etc. by Paul D. White, M.D. and Edward F. Bland, M.D., Boston.

"The treatment consisting primarily of rest with long convalescence and a careful life afterwards, was generally much better carried out in patients who survived than those who died."

The *Sagona's* doctors and nurses were scheduled to land last night, but messages indicated that the men probably would be married aboard the ship, receive first aid treatment and then be taken to St. John's.

He came to Denver from St. Louis shortly after 1900, and had always had good health until he was put under the care of a physician July 17.

Boy, 13, hit by truck on road to recovery.

FELL OFF SECRETARY AND SPRAINED THUMB.

J. Arvil Myers, employee of a Lexington furniture factory, has been awarded medical costs by Industrial Commissioner J. Dewey Dorsett, for injury to his thumb when he fell off a secretary.

New York, Dec. 21 (A.P.) —His face still patched with adhesive plaster, Winston Churchill today was taken to the Waldorf Astoria Hotel and was immediately put to bed under his nurse and with his wife and daughter.

THINGS I WANT RETURNED: Books, *Psycopathia Sexualis*, *Stoddard Pictorial World*, *Customs of Mankind* and a bed pan. These have been loaned and not returned. Please return to Dr. R. C. Taylor.

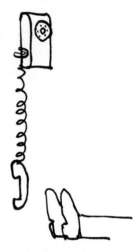

J. W. C., prominent Wichita druggist, a pioneer in Wichita, is recovering from a serious illness at his home, following a relapse caused by the news that his wife was recovering from an operation in Wesley hospital.

WICHITA
EAGLE

Personal

* * *

PERSONAL: Lawyer will read will tomorrow at residence of Edgar Hearn, who died June 19th to accommodate his relatives.

Parisian gentleman, 41, well educated, high feelings, wishes to marry lady, 30 years of age, good temper, sweet, agreeable looking and sufficient personal fortune.

NEW ORLEANS TRIBUNE

PERSONAL: I will not be responsible for any debt that may be incurred by my wife, Katherine Schaefer — DeTemple — Smith — Powell — Ulrucci —O'Mara, she having left my bed and board and now resides between Jean Court, Greenlawn and Huntington Village.
(Signed) Robert O'Mara.

THE HUNTINGTON TIMES

PHILADELPHIA
RECORD

PERSONAL: A young man that has money to burn would like to meet a girl that is a good match.

THE HUNTSVILLE
FORESTER

PERSONAL: If the person who stole my B.V.D.'s off the wash line on the roof will return them at once, no indecent exposure will be made.

NEW YORK
EVENING JOURNAL

Miss Stevens has just announced her engagement to Mr. Twelvetrees. Mr. Twelvetrees is business manager of the Standard Corporation's New York branch office, and Miss Stevens has been working under him.

PERSONAL: WIDOWER, 44, lost wife by death, have four children, would like to meet some working lady, medium size.

THE DENVER POST

PERSONALS PURELY: WANTED wife with $250 to market coal properties, divide profits. Must be musical, unbobbed and religious. Weight 125 pounds, 5 ft. 4 inches. Come at once. Write Mr. L. Aragon, Cleveland, Tenn.

KNOXVILLE NEWS SENTINEL

CAPITAL WANTED: Man losing money in business would like someone to join him.

DENVER POST

PEORIA
JOURNAL

NOTICE: I wish to thank all who so kindly assisted me in the death of my husband.

Widow, still in possession of her late husband's clothes, medium size, would like to meet man whom they would fit, with view to matrimony.

NEW ORLEANS
TRIBUNE

MISCELLANEOUS: EUR-OPEAN is desirous of making the acquaintance with a young and sympathetic "sportswoman" for excursions in auto (far and fast) starting from Saturday afternoon to Sunday night. Friendship and all without any expenses. Write for understandings to P.O. Box 162.

MANILA
DAILY BULLETIN

Mr. & Mrs. J. Brown wish to express thanks to their friends who so kindly assisted at the burning of their residence last night.

BOSTON GLOBE

SAN FRANCISCO
EXAMINER

PERSONAL: Will the gent who spit in my eye last night let me know where I can get a plug of that swell tobacco?

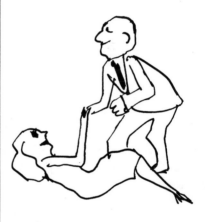

PERSONAL: Will gentleman who picked fallen woman up on Main near Front Street on Monday afternoon, kindly call 4385-J.

DEMOCRAT &
CHRONICLE

Mrs. Sarah Allen is sick at her home at Bayly's Neck and all persons are requested by her sons to stop coming to see the big hog until she improves.

Couple, he personable, she former model 34, 26, 34 seek to meet other couples interested in fun and games.

Birth
Announcements

*   *   *

Dr. C. Dana Carter reports the birth of a daughter to Mr. and Mrs. years ago on account of Mr. Jones'.

CHARLESTON GAZETTE

A son of Mr. and Mrs. Wilson announced his birth yesterday at St. Francis Hospital.

FAR ROCKAWAY JOURNAL

Yesterday we announced that Mr. and Mrs. J. Herman have a baby boy, but due to an error, they are the parents of a girl.

Born to Mr. and Mrs. Sebastian Peluso of 234 Chelsea Avenue, this city, at Monmouth Memorial Hospital, Friday, a son. The Elks plan to run the show again Feb. 28 for the benefit of those who were unable to see Saturday's performance.

LONG BRANCH
DAILY RECORD

Chicago, Feb. 28—Green Cox, a Negro, today became a father for the twenty-ninth time. His first wife bore four children years ago. Lens, his second, is the mother of twenty-five, including three sets of twins. Cox is a house wrecker.

NEW YORK
WORLD-TELEGRAM

GRAND RAPIDS
HERALD

Mr. and Mrs. Lee Brown (Miss Elizabeth Reaves), will be interested to learn that they have a son who was born in a New York hospital Monday afternoon.

ARKANSAS
GAZETTE

Lum Grace, farmer living five miles southwest of here, became a father for the fourteenth time this week.

CLARKSBURG
EXPONENT

Mr. and Mrs. Leonard Mc-Ginness are the parents of a seven pound son born at their home in Howesville on June 13. The child has not been made.

WAYCROSS
JOURNAL-HERALD

Mrs. George Earl, who gave birth to a nine-year-old daughter, is reported as getting along fine. A. J. Dill of Farley, who suffered a broken leg in the same accident, is recovering.

WATKINS PRESS

Mr. and Mrs. Verle Kock of Brighton are the guests of a son born today at the Jefferson County hospital.

Women's Page

* * *

THE NEW YORK
TIMES

Breechettes will be in particular demand; their warmth and their easy-off qualities making them particularly welcome to girls, who must be prepared for the rigors of the afternoon and the exigencies of the evening.

If you will devote one-half hour once a week and five minutes daily to the care of your finger-nails, you can keep them rosy and perfectly groomed. File the nails and remove any rough edges. Soak one hand in warm water while you work on the other.

PHILADELPHIA
LEDGER

The cottage cheese salad is to be made of balls of the cheese, served this time on chicory—so decorative. And Mr. Spratt's balls will be rolled in chopped walnuts, because he likes them that way.

DENVER
POST

When choosing flowers for a dinner table centerpiece, it is always wise to observe the following rule: The centerpiece should be very high, allowing conversational activities beneath it, for both receptacles and flowers should be low enough to permit intercourse between guests.

London dress reformers urge that men discontinue wearing trousers.

Fannie Farmer is more than the deceased author of America's greatest cook book. She is a force. Coming upon a nation wallowing in culinary ignorance and chaos, she gave that chaos some semblance of order and good sense. The modern housewife, with her Fannie to back her up, is ready for anything.

BALTIMORE
SUN

Job Opportunities—
Position Wanted

* * *

NEW YORK
TELEGRAM

WANTED: WORK. Anything will do. I am 26 years old, have wife, two kids, play saxophone in orchestra, but am otherwise respectable.

JOB WANTED: Honest man will take anything.

WANTED: Man and wife as caretakers for a gentleman's country house, one must be sober.

SITUATIONS WANTED: German girl, 24, wants General. 2½ years. Present employer. Pauline's, Davis 7777.

Swedish, 29 wants General. 1 yr. former employer. Pauline's, Davis 7777.

German, 27, wants General. 3 yrs. former employer. Pauline's, Davis 7777.

THE EVANSTON REVIEW

WANTED — SALESGIRL, must be respectable until after Christmas. Apply Box 343.

DALLAS NEWS

NEAT, QUICK girl want-
ed for lunch—

WANTED — situation by
white couple, man as
b u t c h e r, w o m a n a s
trained nurse. Will con-
sider dentist or doctor's
office. Apply Box 6, Lake-
wood, Ohio.

POSITION WANTED:
Nurse, practical, regis-
tered; obstetric cases;
lady patients preferred.
Leeds 1835K11.

COLORED NURSE, post-graduate course in caring for invalids wants position. References. Call Brunson Undertaking Parlor, Florence Villa. Phone 24-832.

GERMAN - AMERICAN wants work around house for room and board. Likes cooking children.

BOOKKEEPER and typist, thoroughly experienced. Prefer one with silk underwear. Tri-Knit, 31 E. 32 D.

WANTED: GIRLS to play ragtime piano. Don't have to be good.

POSITIONS WANTED, WOMEN: Widow, 36, anxious to hear of situation as housekeeper where she could have child as part of salary; references exchanged. Write Christina Rhodes, Pine City, Minn.

HELP WANTED: Farm hand wanted to milk and drive truck.

NORFOLK
LEDGER DISPATCH

WANTED: A strong donkey to do entire work of a country doctor.

ENGLISH
COUNTRYSIDE
WEEKLY

WANTED: FEMALE Impersonator. Must sing, dance and produce. Add 1459J.

RENO REGISTER
AND TRIBUNE

I NEED a young lady un-attached to help develop photos in dark room.

WANTED: An attractive young girl to be my wife and share my frigidaire.

POSITIONS WANTED FE-MALE: Unencumbered widow, not from choice but from calamity, wants a place as housekeeper in a first class motherless home where other servants are retained. Don't want manual labor, but can manage fine. Want good salary with little to do. Lemon pies a specialty and broiled chicken, little salad with it makes a good meal. Please answer at once as I'm in need of money. Can furnish references but don't want to. Press Scimitar, Box 19.

MEMPHIS
PRESS SCIMITAR

WANTED: COOK; one with some Scotch in her preferred. 601 North Main.

For Sale

~~~~~~~~~~~~~~~~~~~~~~~

* * *

COW FOR SALE: Slightly used 1931 Jersey hay-burner, hornless and in wonderful running condition, hits on all fours, self-filling radiator with four good faucets.

GREENVILLE PRESS

FOR SALE: High grade Jersey male. This male's milk tested 8%. Oscar Gaffner. Stone Service Station.

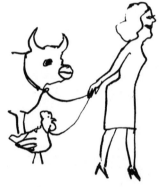

WOMAN wants to sell her chickens, her cow and her ass. Good value.

DENVER POST

FOR SALE: 1 cow by lady with 3 calves.

BUFFALO COURIER-EXPRESS

FOR SALE: Baby carriage. Slightly used. Going out of business.

DENVER POST

FOR SALE: Bicycle by lady slightly used.

DENVER POST

FOR SALE: Twin beds, one just like new.

FOR SALE: A man's bicycle; also a woman's frame and other parts.

ELMIRA
STAR GAZETTE

FOR SALE: Modern six-room residence with bath in center of town. Price reasonable for quick sale.

BLUEFIELD
DAILY TELEGRAPH

FOR SALE: Steinway piano, practically new, property of lady too large for her rooms.

THE HOLLAND
EVENING SENTINEL

BAYSIDE REVIEW

FOR SALE: Large crystal vase by lady slightly cracked. Box No. 500.

LOS ANGELES TIMES

FOR SALE: Complete set of needlework chairs and couch by lady with a broad settee. Box 736M.

PEORIA JOURNAL

BULLDOG FOR SALE. Will eat anything, very fond of children.

MEDINAH WEEKLY

FOR SALE: All rights to wonderful health restoring tonic. Reason for selling, owner just passed away.

FOR SALE: Baker's business, good trade, large oven, owner has been in it for 17 years.

Wanted

* * *

LONDON
DAILY EXPRESS

WANTED TO BUY: One crib in good condition and twin beds.

TRADE HAMMOCK for twin baby carriage. John C. Bell, Sites, California.

PORT ELGIN
TIMES

COMPLETE SET of books *What Every Young Woman Should Know* in original wrappers. Will trade for baby's bath. Box F. 17.

WANTED: ANTIQUE bed by dealer over 300 years old. Box 672M.

WANTED: SAINT BERNARD to mate with my Pekingese. Anxious to reach happy medium.

WANTED: GOOD hunting dog by a Lambertville man 3 years old with good pedigree.

BAMBOO FISHING ROD in exchange for riding breeches for man of 45 with reinforced rear.

Lost and Found

* * *

DENVER POST

LOST. Brown Collie dog. Reward by owner with curly tail.

LIMA STAR

LOST: ½ ANGORA GRAY striped kitten, vicinity Mitchell drugstore, on St. Johns. Rice 7091. Reward.

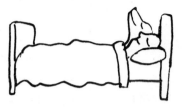

Whoever found my lost dog please return at once, if not please sleep with him as I do. Jill Einstein.

THE
HOUND HERALD

Will party who found pants on Pass Christian road notify Alice Boyd, Handsboro.

Trousers lost between 6140 and 59th and Holmes. Highland 2639.

BILOXI
NEWSPAPER

Woman who lost handbag in State Theatre restroom is heartsick over loss, especially of jewelry which was from her husband of no particular value.

DEARING TIMES

REWARD: For return of $50 check lost between York and Third Avenues, vicinity 73rd St. Urgent as check unsigned. Yorkville Advance, 337 E. 79th St., Box 45.

FOUND: $20. In Green Lake 18 years ago. Owner can have same by identifying the money.

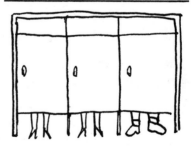

Wrist watch, man's, lost lady's rest rm., Sears Roebuck Co. Lib. rew. MI2896.

FRIEND SENTINEL

LOST: Ladies' underwear on the streets of town. If found return to Sentinel office.

ALBANY HERALD

LOST: Thursday night near Auditorium, flesh-colored silk knickers. Telephone 613. 15-1t.

Apartments
and Houses

*   *   *

CHICAGO TRIBUNE

WILL SHARE 3 rm. apt. Frigid. Lady or man. $15 mo. 3945 Rokeby. Aft. 7 p.m.

TWIN FALLS NEWS

PART OF small house with widow, 1404 8th Ave. East.

NEW YORK TELEGRAM

17TH, 206 E.—Beautifully furnished single room, twin bath. Rice.

NEW HAVEN
JOURNAL-COURIER

TO RENT: One room, good location, near School of Music. Bathroom has good acoustics.

FOR RENT: Nicely furnished front room with mother and daughter. $8 per week for one, $10 for two.

MINNEAPOLIS
CONTEMPORARY

**TEANECK
TIMES-REVIEW**

WRITE FOR rooms. Our inn is located on a delightful bluff and is run accordingly.

Obituary

* * *

The man was killed instantly from being kicked in the stomach by a horse. No bones were broken.

THE HUNTSVILLE
FORESTER

BUFFALO TIMES

Man dies in restaurant while delivering chicken.

DENVER POST

Mark Holland struck a match to see if there was any gasoline in his tank. There was. Aged 49.

Shelby, Dec. 14—Funeral services for John Randolph of Shelby, who died at the home of his sister-in-law, Mrs. Rose Randolph, last Friday were held in Cooper's chapel Monday afternoon. The Rev. Joseph Tuma officiated.

Mr. Randolph was born in Michigan in 1852 and was 75 years with a broken pistol that was harmless.

THE BAYWATER
EVENING WORLD

The man met his death by coming in contact with a live wife.

COLUMBUS
DISPATCH

York, Pa., Oct. 7 (A.P.)—John Holman failed in his attempt to commit suicide, but the coroner says he died trying.

CHAMPAIGN
ILLINOIS

Third Time in Three Months Woman Is Killed by Assailant

~~~~~~~~~~

Mrs. Wallace Probasco, whose husband was found wounded in the apartment of Mrs. R. H. Ingersoll, New York. Mrs. Ingersoll had killed herself before shooting Probasco.

INDIANAPOLIS
STAR

Mr. Ralph Horner returned to work today after an unavoidable absence due to his death.

NORFOLK NEWS

Owing to the lack of space
and the rush of editing
this issue, several births
and deaths will be post-
poned until next week.